D1531181

INCREDIBLE **TRUE** ADVENTURES
LOST IN THE BERMUDA TRIANGLE
AND OTHER MYSTERIES

ANITA GANERI & DAVID WEST

rosen publishing's
rosen central®

New York

Published in 2012 by The Rosen Publishing Group, Inc.
29 East 21st Street, New York, NY 10010

Designed and produced by

David West Books

Designer: Rob Shone
Editor: Katharine Pethick
Illustrator: David West

Picture credits:

9tr, Nuno Nogueira; 9br, Adam Baker; 12t, Ximénex; 12mtr, Masanalv; 12ml, Min-yen Hsu; 12mr, Harris
& Ewing Collection (Library of Congress); 13ml, Ian Sherlock; 13mb, Jensens; 16–17t, Ballista; 16l
Macfarlane, J.; 16m Pierre Denys de Montfort; 17mlb, Kyknoord; 17mr Gulf of Maine Cod Project, NOAA
National Marine Sanctuaries; Courtesy of Natonal Archives; 17tr, 36mrb, NASA; 20m ahisgett; 20tr,
20–21main, SrA Joshua Strang; 21tm, ISUAL Project; 21bl, Julian Kupfer; 24-25main, Geckow; 24bl J S
Henrardi; 25br, Christophe Delaere; 25mr, Wally Pacholka; 28mr, 41br, 44br, Library of Congress; 28–29,
US Air Force Photo; 28tr, Fate magazine; 29mr, US Navy; 29m, Wusel007; 29br NOAA; 36–37b, Cburnett;
37br, D. Roddy (U.S. Geological Survey), Lunar and Planetary Institute; 40–41main, Banana Donuts;
41br, Ebenezer Sibley, 44mr, Willy Stöwer; 44t, Alexander Gardner Library of Congress; 45ml, Dmitry
Rozhkov; 45bl, Jonathan Klinger

Library of Congress Cataloging-in-Publication Data

Ganeri, Anita, 1961-
Lost in the Bermuda Triangle and other mysteries / Anita Ganeri, David West.
p. cm. -- (Incredible true adventures)
Includes bibliographical references and index.
ISBN 978-1-4488-6658-8 (library binding) -- ISBN 978-1-4488-6662-5 (pbk.) -- ISBN 978-1-4488-6670-0
(6-pack)
1. Parapsychology--Juvenile literature. 2. Curiosities and wonders--Juvenile literature. I. West, David. II.
Title.
BF1031.G13 2012
130--dc23

2011031160

Printed in China

CPSIA Compliance Information Batch #DWW12YA:
For further information contact Rosen Publishing, New York, New York, at 1-800-237-9932.

CONTENTS

INTRODUCTION

Huge, ape-like creatures. Lost cities of gold. Ghost ships, UFOs, and monsters living in Loch Ness. For centuries, people have been puzzled and fascinated by famous mysteries like these. Some can be explained by science; others remain unexplained. Their stories make gripping reading as their hidden and baffling facts unfold.

The Pyramids of Giza in Egypt are over 4,000 years old. The tallest, the Pyramid of Cheops, is the most massive structure on Earth. Yet archaeologists are still unsure how the ancient Egyptians built them.

"Spring Heeled Jack, the Terror of London" claims the advertisement for a Victorian Penny Dreadful (an early form of pulp fiction). With fiery eyes, metal claws, and the ability to leap high into the air, Spring Heeled Jack struck terror in the hearts of people throughout England in the nineteenth century. Who or what he was remains a mystery to this day.

FIND OUT MORE

BIGFOOT
"There's something out there and it's moving!"

As he spoke, Fred Beck crept toward the cabin door. It was the middle of the night. Beck and his four companions had been woken from their sleep by a series of loud thuds. Someone, or something, was hurling rocks at the cabin walls.

Peering out through a crack in the wood, Beck could make out three huge, shadowy shapes, over seven feet (2 meters) tall and covered in hair, moving around outside. They were trying to break through the heavy log door. Next thing, the creatures were up on the cabin roof. Immediately the men opened fire. For a while, they held the creatures at bay, but the attacks went on all night.

It was July 1924. The men were miners prospecting for gold in the Muddy River in Washington State. For days, the men had been aware that they were being watched.

One morning, as they got ready to leave, Beck suddenly turned around. Behind him stood a large, ape-like creature. Beck picked up his gun and took aim…

FIND OUT MORE

Strange Beasts

The miners' story spread like wildfire and the hunt was on for the "apemen." The creatures became known as "Bigfoot," after the footprints found at the renamed Ape Canyon. Since then, there have been sightings of Bigfoot and similar creatures, such as Yetis, all over the world.

THE THEORIES

There are many theories about what these ape-like creatures might be. Are they an extinct species of giant ape, or are they descendants of a group of prehistoric hominids (early humans)?

Is Bigfoot an extinct giant ape (below) or a hominid (below left)? Or is it an elaborate hoax?

8

THE EVIDENCE

No one has yet managed to capture a Bigfoot, but plenty of other evidence has been found. Most of this is in the form of footprints, tracks, films, and photographs.

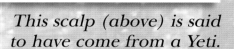

This scalp (above) is said to have come from a Yeti.

This film (right) claims to show a female Bigfoot in California, but is it a fake?

Bigfoot hunters have built large traps (below) to catch them.

A cast (right) of a footprint, claimed to have been made by a Bigfoot. Is the Florida skunk ape (left), named after its terrible smell, also a Bigfoot?

THE LIKELIHOOD

The most likely explanation is that the creatures are actually bears or apes that have been wrongly identified. Despite this, tales of strange beasts continue to haunt people.

A Black bear in dense woodland

THE SEARCH FOR EL DORADO
"Gnnngh! Go, Gonzalo! We will hold them off!"

With these words, the Spanish soldier fell forward into the river, an Indian arrow in his back. He was one of a handful of men, led by conquistador Gonzalo Pizarro, who had spent months fighting their way through the jungle, their dream of finding El Dorado shattered.

When he left his base in Quito, Ecuador, in February 1541, Pizarro had high hopes of finding the fabled Inca city whose walls and streets were said to be lined with gold. Its king was a great warrior, called El Dorado, the "Golden Man." When he reached the valley of Zumaco, a month after setting off, Pizarro was joined by his cousin, Francisco de Orellana. The two men, together with their expedition force of more than 200 Spaniards and 4,000 natives, headed for the foothills of the Andes Mountains. At first, they made good progress, but the going got steadily tougher. Worse still, when they finally reached the other side, there was nothing to see but jungle.

A golden model of the legendary king of Guatavita sailing on his raft.

By now the men were exhausted and supplies of food were running low. Reluctantly, Pizarro was forced to stop and send de Orellana on ahead, with 50 of his men, to find food.

Weeks went past, but de Orellana did not return, and Pizarro's men were dying. With his expedition in tatters and no sign of El Dorado to be found, Pizarro and the remaining 80 men headed home.

The search was later taken up by the Spaniard Don Antonio Sepulveda. In 1580, he reached Lake Guatavita, where it was said an extraordinary ceremony had taken place. Each year, the local king was coated in gold dust and rowed on a raft to the center of the lake while the crowd threw golden offerings into the water. Hoping to find the treasure, Sepulveda tried to drain the lake, but the channel he dug collapsed.

Four hundred years later, a British gold mining firm decided to take up the challenge…

FIND OUT MORE

Lost Places

In 1912, a British firm constructed tunnels to empty the lake. It drained quickly, but, instead of golden treasure, they were left with a bed of mud that set hard like concrete!

Francisco de Orellana (left) joined Gonzalo Pizarro on his expedition. The ceremony held at Lake Guatavita (below), near Bogota in Colombia, gave rise to the legend of El Dorado.

TROY

In the 1870s, German archaeologist Heinrich Schliemann excavated some ruins in Hissarlik, Turkey, that may be the site of the legendary city of Troy (right).

The ancient ruins of Troy in Turkey

Even the invading Spanish never found the ancient Inca city of Machu Picchu (below). It was discovered in 1911 by American archaeologist Hiram Bingham (above), but the reason why it was abandoned remains a mystery.

ATLANTIS

According to legend, Atlantis was an ancient island kingdom that sank without trace thousands of years ago. But did Atlantis ever actually exist?

Akrotiri (left) was a town on the Greek island of Thera, now called Santorini (below). Could Thera have been the location for Atlantis and could its towns have looked like Akrotiri?

Many places claim to be Camelot, the lost castle and court associated with the legendary King Arthur (above left). They include Tintagel in Cornwall, England (above right).

In 79 CE, the Roman town of Pompeii was buried under volcanic ash. Eventually, its location and even its name were forgotten until its ruins (left) were discovered in 1748.

THE LOCH NESS MONSTER
"Och no, the legend is *true*–it is the monster!"

As he picked himself up off the ground, Arthur Grant could not believe his eyes. In front of him rose a huge creature with a long neck and tail. It turned its head to look at Grant, then disappeared into the dark waters of Loch Ness.

Grant, a veterinary student, was riding home early one morning in January 1934, when the massive monster slithered across the road in front of him, headed toward the Loch. Swerving to avoid it, Grant fell off his motorbike. Unhurt, Grant continued on his way home, eager to tell his story.

Grant was not the first person to see the monster. There had been many sightings reported over hundreds of years but since the lake-shore road had been built the previous year, the sightings had become more frequent. Soon, monster-hunters were arriving from all over the world to track down the creature.

In 1970, an American scientist used hydrophones to make underwater recordings of many sounds that couldn't be explained away by known aquatic creatures. Then, later in the 1970s, another team of American scientists took photographs showing what looked like a giant flipper. Was this finally proof that the Loch Ness Monster was real?

FIND OUT MORE

Lake and Sea Monsters

The photographs were sent to many leading scientists in the United Kingdom. Some believed that they showed a monster; others were not convinced. The search for the Loch Ness Monster was set to continue...

Could "Nessie" be a plesiosaur (below), a long-necked reptile thought to be extinct?

The Bunyip is a mythical Australian lake monster.

The Kraken (left) is a legendary sea monster, but it may have been based on sightings of the real-life giant squid. Unlike the Kraken, sea serpents (below) were depicted with snake-like bodies.

SEA SERPENTS

There have been sightings of mysterious monsters in lakes and seas around the world. Serpent-like sea monsters were often reported by sailors, but it is most likely that these were cases of mistaken identity.

THE USUAL SUSPECTS

One explanation for lake monsters is that they might be animals, such as whales and basking sharks—or waves and waterspouts—distorted by the lake water.

The bodies of giant squid (above and left) are sometimes found washed up on beaches or caught in fishing nets.

Seen beneath the water, the shapes of a large seal (left) or fish (above) could look like a monster.

Are strange blobs of matter called globsters (right) found washed up on shores unidentified sea creatures, or are they the remains of whales and sharks?

THE MYSTERY OF BALL LIGHTNING
"Look out! That light, it's heading straight for you!"

As he shouted the warning, the man could see that it was already too late. The strange ball of white and blue light, which was about to knock him unconscious, had already hit his colleague on the forehead, killing him instantly. The dead man was Professor George Richmann, a brilliant scholar and head of the physics department at the Academy of Sciences in St. Petersburg, Russia, who was carrying out pioneering work in electricity. Inspired by Benjamin Franklin's recent experiments into the nature of lightning, Richmann had invented a device for attracting lightning during a storm. A wire was attached to the top of his house, leading down to an iron bar inside.

It was August 6, 1753, and the experiment was underway, when the ball of fire appeared and struck Richmann. The unfortunate professor had become the first person to be killed by a mysterious phenomenon, known as ball lightning.

A telephone that has been struck by lightning.

But, Richmann's wasn't the first close encounter. On October 21, 1638, a church in Devon, England, was almost destroyed by a large ball of fire, which smashed pews and windows during afternoon service, and filled the building with thick, dark, foul-smelling smoke. Four people died and many others were injured.

Many more accounts followed. Natural ball lightning is unpredictable and appears only infrequently. It has even been seen inside submarines and on board aircraft. In 1984, the passengers and crew of a Russian aircraft had the fright of their lives while flying across the Black Sea during a thunderstorm. A glowing ball of light appeared in the cockpit, then disappeared, only to re-emerge in the cabin where it floated slowly over the heads of the stunned passengers.

The question is: what is ball lightning and how does it happen?

FIND OUT MORE

Weird Stuff

Experts agree that ball lightning is linked to electricity, but there is still no widely accepted explanation of what it actually is. Here are some of the theories.

The glow from the aurora borealis (right), plasma lamps (below), and ball lightning is caused by plasma, a type of matter that gives off light.

Foo fighters (below) were mysterious balls of light seen by pilots in World War II.

AERIAL ANOMALIES

Ball lightning might be explained by strange weather phenomena high in the atmosphere, such as St. Elmo's fire (left). This is a type of bluish-green lightning that clings to ships' masts and the wingtips of aircraft.

Could St. Elmo's fire (left) and ball lightning be the same phenomenon?

Could ball lightning explain will-o'-the-wisp (below), ghostly lights often seen over marshes and bogs?

Sprites (above) are flashes of electricity that happen high up in thunderclouds. They include red sprites, blue jets, and elves.

STRANGE RAINS

Apart from ball lightning, many other mysterious weather events have been reported. In 2001, red rain fell in Kerala, India, and there are many accounts of animals and other strange objects falling from the sky.

Another possible explanation for will-o'-the-wisp is bioluminescence–light produced by living things.

Could a waterspout (right) suck up fish which then fall in the rain?

Raining cats and dogs? There have been many showers of fish and frogs.

THE ROSWELL INCIDENT

"One thing's for sure, they're not from *this* world..."

As the man stared down at the ground, shivers ran down his spine. The ghostly, wide-eyed body was like nothing he had ever seen before. With its large head and pale, hairless skin, it was definitely not human, but what else could the creature be?

All around lay hunks of twisted metal. Clearly, some sort of craft had crash landed. Quickly, Major Jesse Marcel, of the Roswell Army Air Field, ordered the site to be cleared. No one was to know about this. If any of the men were asked, they had seen nothing.

Days before, strange lights had been sighted in the skies above Roswell, New Mexico. Then, eyewitnesses reported seeing one of them come crashing down. Was it an alien spacecraft? The news spread like wildfire. On July 8, 1947, anxious to keep the exact site secret, the US Air Force issued a press release confirming the rumor—they had recovered a crashed "flying disk."

Meanwhile, the mystery of the "alien" creature remained. In total secrecy, the body was taken to Roswell Air Base, where it was kept in a hangar. Later, in the base infirmary, an autopsy was carried out.

In the following years, the Roswell Incident was declared dead. Witnesses were silenced and evidence suppressed. Would the American people ever know the truth?

FIND OUT MORE

Close Encounters

I t was finally revealed that the US military had indeed covered up the truth about Roswell. The crashed object was in fact a top-secret surveillance balloon, and not a UFO. As for the alien? There is no evidence that it had ever existed.

The local newspaper (right) printed the UFO story.

General Roger Ramey (left) with part of the debris from the balloon

Area 51 (below) is a secret US military base in Nevada. Some people who believe the Roswell story also believe crashed alien spacecraft are kept here.

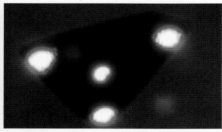

For centuries, mysterious lights have been seen in the sky. A 1561 German illustration shows an aerial battle (top). Are these the lights of alien spaceships (above)?

STRANGE LIGHTS

There have been thousands of reports of UFOs, but are any of them actually "flying saucers?" The phrase was coined by American pilot Kenneth Arnold, who claimed to have seen a formation of UFOs in the sky in 1947.

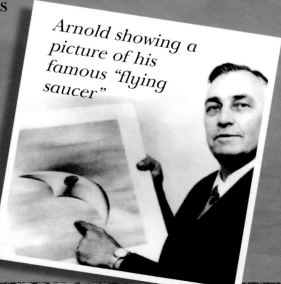

Arnold showing a picture of his famous "flying saucer"

MIFOs AND HOAXES

Most UFOs can be put down to tricks of the weather or wrongly identified aircraft, satellites, and even planets (MIstakenFOs). But some are known to be faked— hoax sightings and abductions, or fake photographs.

Spacecraft, space travel, and aliens have always been popular subjects for fiction.

A reconstruction of the alien figure (below), said to have been discovered at Roswell. Was it based on a real extraterrestrial?

ALL NEW AMAZING SPACE ADVENTURES!
PLANET Comics
PLANET COMICS

SANDHOGS OF MARS

HIJACK ON ALPHA 7
SPACE RANGERS
INVADERS FROM ALTURO

Was this 1952 photograph (above), taken in New Jersey, a fake?

The planet Venus (above right) and lenticular clouds (right) may be mistaken for UFOs. Are crop circles (left) messages from aliens or fakes?

25

LOST IN THE BERMUDA TRIANGLE

"Zzzzzt...calling tower. This is an emergency. We seem to be lost."

Flight leader Lieutenant Charles Taylor's voice sounded strained, and the radio operator back at Fort Lauderdale had trouble making out his words. As the operator tried to find out Taylor's position, it became clear that Taylor and the rest of Flight 19 were in trouble. Seconds later, Taylor could be heard again. Then the radio went dead…

A few hours earlier, at 2:00 p.m., the five US Navy torpedo bombers of Flight 19 set off from Fort Lauderdale, Florida. It was December 5, 1945. The weather was good, and the routine training flight, which would take them out over the Atlantic Ocean before returning to the naval base, should have lasted for around two hours.

At first, everything went as planned. The planes reached the area known as the Hens and Chickens Shoals, and started bombing practice. A short time later, they began to turn west for the second part of the test. At 3:45 p.m., the first signs of trouble appeared, and problems with the planes' compasses were reported. It was hard to establish radio communications on the training frequency because of atmospheric interference. Becoming ever more disoriented, it wasn't long before the pilots were hopelessly lost.

A last radio message was heard at 7:00 p.m., and two seaplanes were sent out from Fort Lauderdale to search for Flight 19. Air bases, aircraft, and merchant ships were also alerted.

Meanwhile, the stricken pilots were still miles from land with no idea which direction they were heading in. They had no choice but to keep flying for as long as their fast-dwindling fuel supplies lasted…

FIND OUT MORE

Lost at Sea

The search for Flight 19 continued for another five days, but no sign or wreckage was ever found. Had the bombers become the latest craft to disappear in the notorious stretch of ocean, known as the Bermuda Triangle?

The story of Flight 19 appeared in the October issue of a magazine called Fate (above).

In 1492, on his voyage to America, Christopher Columbus (above) reported seeing strange lights on the horizon while sailing through the triangle.

BERMUDA

Last known position of Flight 19

FLORIDA

THE BERMUDA TRIANGLE

PUERTO RICO

DEVIL'S TRIANGLE

The area known as the Bermuda, or Devil's, Triangle is a stretch of the Atlantic Ocean with its three points in Bermuda, Miami, and Puerto Rico. Thousands of ships and planes have gone missing in the area in the last few hundred years.

Argosy magazine (above) made the first mention of the "Bermuda Triangle" phrase.

CONNECTING THE DOTS

Explanations of what happens to ships and planes in the Triangle range from alien abductions to black holes. It is more likely that human error or dangerous weather and sea conditions are to blame. The inexperienced flight leader of Flight 19 may simply have taken a wrong turn—but why was no wreckage found?

The USS Cyclops vanished in 1918 with the loss of 306 passengers and crew. She may have been in the Triangle when she sank.

In 1991, a Grumman Cougar jet, like the one here, disappeared from radar screens while flying over the Triangle. No debris was ever found.

In 1948, a DC-3 aircraft (left) disappeared on a flight from Puerto Rico to Miami.

Could rogue waves (right) be to blame for the loss of ships in the Bermuda Triangle? Or could bubbles from frozen methane gas on the seabed (above right) be the cause?

MYSTERY OF THE *MARY CELESTE*

"*Vanished*—the whole crew, as if taken by the wind."

As he spoke, Oliver Deveau shook his head in puzzlement. He had searched every inch of the ship, from stem to bow, but there wasn't a soul on board. The ship was in perfect condition, but the whole crew had vanished, without a trace.

It was December 5, 1872. Deveau was chief mate on the *Dei Gratia*, a British ship sailing across the North Atlantic. When a lookout spotted a ship in trouble, heading toward the Straits of Gibraltar, Deveau and two shipmates rowed over to help.

The name of the stricken ship was the *Mary Celeste.* Launched in Canada in 1861, rumor had it that this 102-foot (31 meters) brigantine was jinxed. Tragedy struck when her first captain fell ill and died, and, from then on, disaster followed disaster. In November 1872, she was sailing from New York, bound for Genoa in Italy, when disaster struck once more.

On board, Deveau searched frantically for any sign of life, but the *Mary Celeste* was like a ghost ship. Strangely, in the sailors' quarters, the crew's belongings were still in place. Stranger still, the captain's table was laid with the remains of his breakfast. It was as though the whole crew had suddenly decided to abandon ship. But where had they gone?

FIND OUT MORE

The Missing

The crew of the *Mary Celeste* was never found and the mystery of the ship remains. But they were not the only people to go missing without trace...

A story by Arthur Conan Doyle (above), about the Mary Celeste *(left), mixed fact with a large dose of fiction.*

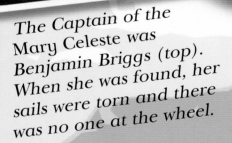

The Captain of the Mary Celeste was Benjamin Briggs (top). When she was found, her sails were torn and there was no one at the wheel.

ANOTHER GHOST SHIP

The schooner, *Carroll A. Deering* (right), ran aground off Cape Hatteras, North Carolina, in 1921. When rescuers finally boarded the ship, they found that her crew had mysteriously and suddenly disappeared. An investigation was launched by the US government, but the mystery was never solved.

Some people suspected that first mate Charles McLellan murdered the captain of the Carroll A. Deering *(above) and ran the ship aground.*

Into the Blue

Many aircraft and their crews have disappeared in mysterious circumstances. American pilot Amelia Earhart (right) vanished in 1937 as she attempted to fly around the world.

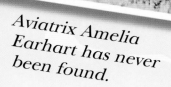

Aviatrix Amelia Earhart has never been found.

In 1956, a B-47 Stratojet (above) disappeared while flying over the Mediterranean Sea. Despite search efforts, no debris or crash site was ever found.

The Lost Colony

The Roanoke Colony was an English settlement established in the 1580s on Roanoke Island in North Carolina. In 1590, the settlement was found to be deserted, with no trace of the people who had lived there. It is still not certain where they might have gone.

In 1900, the three lighthouse keepers on Eilean Mor (above), an island off the Scottish coast, mysteriously disappeared. Ten years earlier, in 1890, Louis Le Prince (right) boarded a train in Dijon, France, and was never seen again.

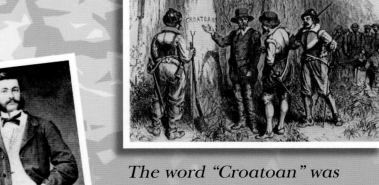

The word "Croatoan" was carved on a tree trunk (above). Did this mean that the Roanoke settlers had joined the local Croatan Native Americans?

THE TUNGUSKA EVENT
"Two suns——why are there two suns?"

Shielding their eyes from the blinding light, the couple stared at the sky in disbelief. Seconds later, a massive explosion threw them to the ground. All around them, rocks and trees were falling. Was this the end of the world?

It was June 30, 1908. In the remote Tunguska region of Siberia, another hot, dry day was just beginning. Suddenly, a huge ball of bluish light flashed across the cloudless sky, leaving a trail of smoke behind it. Then the ball exploded, with a bang like gun fire.

The couple were not the only people to witness this extraordinary event. One man described seeing the sky split in two, then cover the forest in fire. By now, the heat was so ferocious, it felt like his shirt was on fire. Above, great claps of thunder rumbled and a howling, hot wind blew the man off his feet. Then, the earth itself began to move, shaking the trees and buildings.

The explosion ripped through the forest, flattening millions of trees over a huge area of land. And for weeks afterward the skies above the village of Tunguska glowed with light, even at night.

But what had really happened on that fateful morning? Were local people right? Did the explosion mark the beginning of the end of the world?

FIND OUT MORE

Deep Impacts

The cause of the Tunguska event is still debated. Some people believed that a UFO had exploded or that a black hole had passed over the Earth. The experts had other ideas...

The first scientist to reach the devastated area (above) was Leonid Kulik (above left). It is estimated that the blast knocked down 80 million trees over an area of around 770 square miles (2,000 sq. km.).

Was the exploding object a comet (top) or an asteroid (above)? The debate continues.

SMALL OBJECT IMPACTORS

Many scientists believe that the explosion may have been caused by an asteroid or meteorite bursting apart in the air. In the 1990s, researchers found particles of materials trapped in tree resin. These materials are commonly found in asteroids.

The force of the explosion was roughly equal to the biggest ever US nuclear test in 1954.

COUNTDOWN TO DOOMSDAY

Around 65 million years ago, many species of plants and animals, including the dinosaurs, became extinct. Most experts agree that this mass extinction was caused by a giant meteorite crashing into the Earth. Could another impact spell doomsday for the planet?

In 1994, a comet struck the planet Jupiter. Marks showing where the comet hit could be seen for many months.

Special instruments measuring the seabed have shown a huge crater (above) off the Yucatan coast in Central America. The impact (right) from the meteor that made it could have wiped out most of the life on Earth.

Meteor Crater in Arizona is 4,000 feet (1,200 meters) in diameter and was made by a meteor measuring 150 feet (45 meters) across.

A GHOSTLY WARNING

"Wh-who are you? What do you want?"

Lord Dufferin's voice shook as he spoke these words. As the shadowy figure in front of him turned, Dufferin found himself recoiling in horror. The face he was looking at was so hideous, it was surely not human?

A diplomat and adventurer, Dufferin was staying at a friend's old manor house near Tullamore, in Ireland. One night, he was woken up by noises in the garden outside. Looking out of the window, he saw a mysterious, hooded figure carrying a large box on his back. The figure looked up at him and stared for a moment before continuing on his way across the lawn. Thinking it must be a burglar, Dufferin went outside to investigate. As he got closer, he noticed that the box was a coffin.

Next morning, Dufferin told his friend what had happened. Both men were mystified but decided they should put the experience down to a bad dream.

Some years later, Lord Dufferin was attending a diplomatic function at the Grand Hotel in Paris. Along with several of his companions, he crossed the lobby to the newly-installed elevator, the hotel's pride and joy.

As the elevator doors opened, Dufferin let out a loud gasp. The lift operator was the same man he had seen all those years before in Ireland! Dufferin stepped back in shock, startling his companions, who had noticed nothing wrong. Then he waved the elevator to go on without them. Seconds later, the lift cables broke and the elevator plummeted to the ground, killing everyone inside.

An investigation launched into the accident revealed that the lift operator had only been hired that morning, while the regular operator was out sick. But who was the mysterious man?

FIND OUT MORE

The Spirit World

Nobody ever identified the lift operator who saved Lord Dufferin's life by warning him away from the elevator, and Dufferin remained convinced that he had seen a ghost. Surely there was no other explanation?

Lord Dufferin (right) enjoyed telling his ghost story to friends, even though some of them doubted that he was telling the truth!

THINGS THAT GO BUMP

Ghosts are said to be the souls of the dead who return to the world of the living. Some return to take revenge on those who have harmed them. Others bring warnings of disaster or death.

Is this famous picture of a ghostly figure on the stairs a trick of photography?

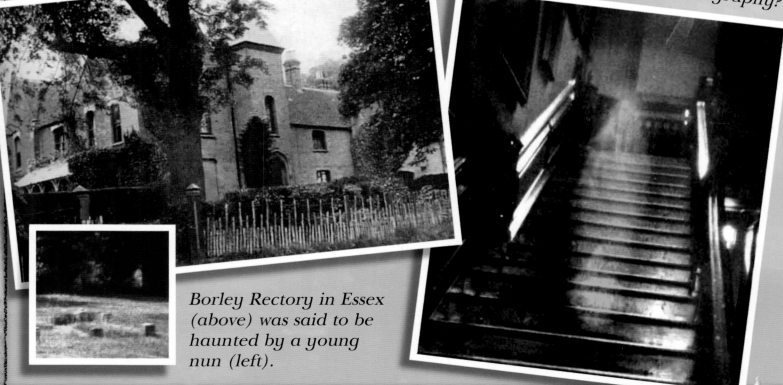

Borley Rectory in Essex (above) was said to be haunted by a young nun (left).

MEDIUM IS THE MESSAGE

Do ghosts really exist? Many people think so. Others believe that ghostly sightings are more likely to be tricks of the imagination or of photography. Hauntings, too, can be faked using theatrical costumes and trickery.

Are ghosts called poltergeists (left) responsible for things that "go bump in the night"?

Magicians summon the spirit of a dead woman (above) in order to gain knowledge.

Does ectoplasm really disguise a ghostly form, or is it simply a medium's trick?

A ghost hunter (above) holding an EMF (electromagnetic field) meter

Famous escape artist Harry Houdini (left and above) spent much of his time exposing fake mediums and psychics.

PRECOGNITION
"No! No—don't..."

As John Williams watched, a distinguished-looking man in a blue coat and white waistcoat entered the lobby of the House of Commons in London, England, flanked by Members of Parliament. He was none other than Spencer Perceval, the British Prime Minister. Moments later, Williams saw another man enter the lobby, dressed in a brown coat with gold buttons. To Williams's horror, the man drew out a small pistol and fired it straight at the Prime Minister, who fell to the ground as blood spread across his waistcoat. Immediately, several men grabbed hold of the murderer.

At that moment, Williams sat up in bed in horror, sweat glistening on his face. Waking his wife, he told her what had happened, but she reassured him that he'd only had a bad dream. Still feeling uneasy, Williams went back to sleep, only to have exactly the same dream again. Once again his wife reassured him when he woke up, but, having fallen asleep a second time, the dream was again repeated.

Next day, Williams was haunted by his dream and wondered what he should do. Should he leave his home in Cornwall and travel to London to warn the Prime Minister, or would he just be branded a madman? Surely no one would take him seriously. Having discussed the matter with several friends in town, he decided to stay at home, but he scanned the newspapers anxiously for any news from the Houses of Parliament in Westminster.

A week or so later, on May 11, 1812, Spencer Perceval left the Prime Minister's residence. Because it was such a fine day, he decided he would walk the short distance to the House of Commons.

At around 5:15 p.m., Perceval entered the lobby of the Houses of Parliament. Just seconds later, a man called John Bellingham, dressed in a brown coat with gold buttons, stepped out from behind a pillar, drew a pistol from his clothes and…

FIND OUT MORE

Mind Power

…shot the Prime Minister dead! The assassination happened exactly as John Williams had dreamt. Was this simply a matter of coincidence? Or does the human mind truly have the power to foresee events in the future?

US President Abraham Lincoln (left) dreamt he had died ten days before his assassination. Several passengers on the Titanic (below) had premonitions that the ship was going to sink.

SIXTH SENSE

Sensing something without using the normal five senses is known as "sixth sense," or ESP (extra-sensory perception). Precognition —knowing what is going to happen in the future—is one aspect of this mysterious phenomenon.

Among other predictions, 16th-century Frenchman Michel de Nostredame (above; better known as Nostradamus) foresaw the rise of Hitler (right) and the Nazis.

Paranormals

Other areas of the paranormal include telepathy and clairvoyance. Telepathy is sensing what people are thinking or feeling, by ESP. Clairvoyance is sensing things happening via ESP.

Mediums sometimes use a crystal ball to see into the future (right). This is called scrying.

In medieval Europe, tarot cards (above) were used to play card games. Later they were used by fortune tellers.

By studying the movement of the planets through the sky (below), astrologers claim to be able to predict the future.

Uri Geller (above) claims to be able to bend metal utensils (above). He does not touch them but uses the power of his mind alone.

In a famous experiment to test telepathic skills, one person (left) is cut off from the normal senses of sight, hearing, smell, touch, and taste. Zener cards (right) are also used to test mind reading abilities.

ALEXANDER
CRYSTAL·SEER

KNOWS SEES TELLS ALL

GLOSSARY

Abduction When a person is taken by force.

Archaeologist A person who studies ancient places and objects.

Assassination When an important political person is murdered.

Brigantine A two-masted sailing ship.

Conquistador The Spanish word for conqueror. The conquistadors were the Spanish soldiers who invaded Central and South America in the 16th century.

Extinction The process of a group of living creatures dying out.

Hominid An early human being.

Hydrophones Instruments that convert sound traveling through water into electrical signals.

Lenticular Shaped like a curved lens.

Loch A lake.

Meteorite A rock-like object from space that enters the Earth's atmosphere.

Paranormal Something that cannot be explained normally.

Parliament In the United Kingdom, it is made up of the sovereign, the House of Lords, and the House of Commons.

Plesiosaur A long-necked prehistoric sea reptile.

Prime Minister The head of an elected government; a chief minister.

Surveillance Surveillance equipment is used to keep a person or a group of people under observation.

UFOs Unidentified flying objects.

Veterinary The study of animal medicine.

FURTHER INFORMATION

ORGANIZATIONS AND WEB SITES

International UFO Museum and
Research Center
114 North Main Street
Roswell, NM 88203
(800) 822 - 3524
Web site:
http://www.roswellufomuseum.com

Bigfoot Discovery Museum
5497 Highway 9
Felton, CA 95018
Web site:
http://www.bigfootdiscovery
project.com

Meteor Crater Enterprises, Inc.
Interstate 40, Exit 233
Winslow, AZ 86047
(800) 289 - 5898
Web site:
http://www.meteorcrater.com

FOR FURTHER READING

Budd, Deena West. *The Weiser Guide to Cryptozoology: Werewolves, Dragons, Skyfish, Lizard Men, and Other Fascinating Creatures Real and Mysterious.* San Francisco, CA: Weiser Books, 2010.

Jeffrey, Gary and Moulder, Bob. *Graphic Mysteries: The Loch Ness Monster and Other Lake Mysteries.* New York, NY: Rosen Publishing, 2006.

Hawes, Jason, and Grant Wilson. *Ghost Hunt: Chilling Tales of the Unknown.* New York, NY: Little, Brown Books for Young Readers, 2010.

Shone, Rob and Spender, Nick. *Graphic Mysteries: Bigfoot and Other Strange Beasts.* New York, NY: Rosen Publishing, 2006.

West, David and Lacey, Mike. *Graphic Mysteries: The Bermuda Triangle, Strange Happenings at Sea.* New York, NY: Rosen Publishing, 2006.

INDEX

WEB SITES

Due to the changing nature of Internet links, Rosen Publishing has developed an online list of Web sites realtated to the subject of this book. This site is updated regularly.
Please use this link to access this list: http://www.rosenlinks.com/ita/btri